Listen up, schnitzel lover!

You're sitting there with my b
Hopefully you're ready to be l
schnitzel world, because that'

Let me introduce myself: I'm Bjørn. My passion for schnitzels started many years ago – back when the Nokia 3310 was the hottest thing on the market, and you still used a modem to get online. Remember that sound? I was on a trip to Germany with my friend, and we were hungry as wolves after a long day of sightseeing. And then it happened: We stepped into a small, cozy restaurant with checkered tablecloths and dim lighting, and there, in the middle of the menu, it sat: The German schnitzel. It was love at first bite! Crispy, golden brown, and juicy – I was sold!

You might be thinking, what's so special about a schnitzel? Well, let me tell you! The German schnitzel is a completely different experience than the Danish version. It's like comparing a Lada to a Lamborghini. Both can drive, but the Lamborghini is still a bit nicer, right? The German schnitzel is made with love and care, and it's always perfectly breaded and fried to perfection. The Danish version? Well, it can be a bit dry and boring in comparison. Anyway, back to the story. My friend and I are two history nerds who love exploring Europe's battlefields and bunkers. We're on a mission to find the best schnitzels in every corner of the continent – from Berlin to Vienna, from Hamburg to Munich. And believe me, we've tasted a lot! We've eaten schnitzels as big as our heads, schnitzels with all kinds of fillings, and schnitzels served with the most amazing sauces.

This book is the culmination of our schnitzel odyssey. Here you'll find everything you need to know about this breaded delicacy – from the best recipes to the most interesting stories. So read, learn, and be inspired! Maybe you'll even find the courage to go on your own schnitzel journey?

P.S. Remember plenty of lemon and potato salad! And a nice cold beer, of course.

Picture this: Tönning, Northern Germany. Hunger strikes. We spot "Restaurant Roter Hahn" and think, "Schnitzel-burger? We gotta try that!"

Expectations high: juicy beef patty in a crispy schnitzel suit. The reality? A culinary gut punch! The patty was classic, but the bun... oh, the bun! A breaded, deep-fried meat-creation that defied gravity and all common sense.

Heavenly? Yes! Heavy? Absolutely! We rolled out of there with a smile and a serious food coma. Roter Hahn, you're crazy! But we love you for it!

Ah, Neumünster! Home of the legendary Autobahn schnitzel – a German classic that makes even the most hardcore speed demon slam on the brakes and pull over.

But this wasn't just any schnitzel. No, it was crowned with a lavish portion of "Gypsy sauce" – an Eastern European-inspired flavor bomb that made our mouths water with its generous amounts of onions and paprika.

Imagine the aroma of paprika mingling with the crispy breading, while the onions play a sweet and sour melody in the background. A true feast for the taste buds that made us forget all about speed limits and just enjoy the moment.

"Gypsy sauce" – a name that might not be entirely politically correct, but hey, the taste certainly isn't lacking anything

Helmstedt, a charming gem in former East Germany, held a culinary surprise in its cozy Ratskeller. Here, in the heart of the city, we devoured not one, but two divine schnitzels that sent our taste buds into overdrive.

The first schnitzel was a symphony of crispy breading, tender meat, and a fried egg flirting mischievously with crispy cubes of bacon. A true classic that made us hum with delight.

The second schnitzel was a more daring affair – a creamy Camembert cheese melted sensually over the golden breading, creating a heavenly alliance of flavor and texture.

Ratskeller in Helmstedt, you know your schnitzel art!

Bad Harzburg, an idyllic spot in the Harz mountains, held a sweat-inducing secret. In the heart of the small town, we found Bräustüb'l, a restaurant promising culinary adventures. But alas, that evening the temperature had risen to unprecedented heights, and sweat trickled down our foreheads as we waited for our meal.

And then it arrived: Schlemmerschnitzel! A true feast for the gods that made us forget all about the heatwave. Crispy breading, tender meat, and a lavish gravy that made our taste buds dance.

"Mums" is all I can say! We ate with gusto, while beads of sweat dripped onto our plates. An unforgettable experience that proved good food can conquer even the most intense heat

Bad Harzburg, you little charmer! Not only do you hide sweat-inducing schnitzel adventures in hidden alleys, you also serve up classics right in the middle of the town square!

Like a shining diamond in a box of cobblestones, we found it: the Wiener-art schnitzel! A crispy, golden beauty, sunbathing on a bed of crispy fries, adorned with a fresh slice of lemon.

A true Viennese classic that made us forget all about the breathtaking scenery of the Harz mountains. We sat there, in the heart of the city, and savored every bite of that heavenly schnitzel.

Simplicity at its finest - and proof that sometimes it's the classic virtues that hit the spot!

Oh, the German Sunday! Everything is closed. Even the most industrious bees take a break. Hunger rumbles, and despair spreads. What to do?

Fear not, dear friends! For even in the Bavarian town of Landshut, on a sleepy Sunday afternoon, there is hope. The Aral gas station, our unexpected savior!

Here, amongst the petrol pumps and motor oil, we found it: the "Quickie"! A humble little sandwich that hid a surprisingly big taste experience. A crispy schnitzel, nestled in a soft flute with a kiss of ketchup. Simple, yes, but oh so effective!

Who would have thought that a gas station could satisfy hunger and save the day? Quickie, you are a true hero in disguise

Salzburg, the city of Mozart, Mirabell Gardens, and... Zum Zirkelwirt! In this charming restaurant, we stumbled upon a schnitzel that was worthy of a masterpiece.

But wait! What's this? Boiled potatoes? Yes, you read that right! A rarity in schnitzel-land, but a welcome change from the eternal french fries.

And as if that wasn't enough, there was also a dollop of homemade redcurrant jam on the side. An unexpected but ingenious combination that made our taste buds sing.

Zum Zirkelwirt, you have taken the schnitzel experience to new heights! Mozart would be proud.

Vienna, Vienna, you beautiful schnitzel mecca! Here, in the heart of the Austrian Empire, we found Schnitzel Wirt - an institution that takes its schnitzel art seriously.

And let me say this right away: The schnitzels here are not for the faint of heart. They are gigantic! Like mill wheels that cover the entire plate and threaten to topple glasses and cutlery.

But fear not, for there is no unnecessary decoration here. No frills or confusing sauces. Just an honest, breaded beauty that speaks for itself.

A pure schnitzel feast that makes the angels sing and the stomach rejoice. Schnitzel Wirt, you are masters of the noble art of serving schnitzels in a class of their own!

Ah, Denmark, you wonderful country! Here, the schnitzel is not just a schnitzel. It's a national hero, a culinary institution, a childhood friend.

And here, served with love, it is in all its glory: The Danish schnitzel! Crispy and golden, surrounded by an army of roasted potatoes, drowned in a velvety smooth gravy, and decorated with an emerald green pea garland.

But wait! What is that mysterious creature hiding on top? A "dreng"! A unique Danish creation consisting of anchovies, capers, and grated horseradish, which gives the schnitzel an extra kick.

A true flavor bomb that sends you straight back to Grandma's kitchen. The Danish schnitzel - a classic that never goes out of style!

Bremen, oh Bremen! Not only known for its musical stray dogs, but also for its ability to serve a schnitzel that sings! At Paulaner's an der Schlachte, with the beautiful Weser River as a backdrop, we devoured this little Wiener-art wonder.

A classic beauty, crispy and golden, basking on the plate. The perfect end to a day filled with adventures in this charming city.

With a view of the river and a schnitzel in our stomachs, we felt like the kings of Bremen. Paulaner's, you know how to spoil a hungry traveler!

After a monotonous drive along Bremen's rather uninspiring entrance road, a bright spot suddenly appeared! Like an oasis in a desert of dull facades, there it stood: Restaurant Feldschlösschen!

With joyful anticipation, we threw ourselves at the menu, which was brimming with temptations. But the choice was easy: Schnitzel, of course! Our eyes fell on the seductive Jägerschnitzel, with its steaming mixture of mushrooms and onions.

And wow, what a portion! The plate was filled to the brim with a crispy, golden schnitzel, drowned in an aromatic mushroom sauce. A true feast for the eyes - and for the palate! We ate until we were about to burst, and rolled out of there with a blissful smile on our lips. Feldschlösschen, you are a true miracle on an otherwise boring entrance road!

Ah, Wunstorf! Yet another charming German provincial town that upholds the noble tradition: the Ratskeller! For what is a German town without a cozy basement restaurant where you can enjoy a good schnitzel in historic surroundings?

And Wunstorf does not disappoint! Here, in the beautiful, vaulted rooms, we enjoyed a schnitzel with mushrooms that made the angels sing. A crispy, golden beauty, covered in a creamy mushroom sauce that made our taste buds dance.

As we sat there enjoying our meal, surrounded by the spirit of history, we felt transported to a bygone era. Wunstorf, you have truly captured the magic of the Ratskeller!

Dortmund, you glorious city of yellow and black! Imagine: We're standing in one of the city's charming squares, in the shadow of the majestic cathedral. Suddenly, a sign catches our attention: "Restaurant Wenkers". Curious, we step inside, and there, in the middle of the menu, awaits a culinary surprise: A schnitzel platter for two!

For two? No, for two or more! Six small schnitzels, each with its own unique sauce, surrounded by braised onions, grilled vegetables, crispy potatoes and Brauhaus chips. A true Schnitzel paradise!
We ravenously attacked this feast, and our taste buds rejoiced. Each schnitzel was a taste sensation in itself, and the side dishes were the perfect symphony to this schnitzel orchestra. Full and happy, we rolled out of the restaurant, ready to conquer the rest of Dortmund!

Hannover, you surprised us! Not only do you have a fantastic town hall that looks like a castle from a Disney movie, you also hide a schnitzel gem with a twist!

Das Zwiespalt, with its funky decor and creative menu, lured us into a world of taste experiences. And here, in the midst of this culinary wonderland, we found it: a schnitzel with cheese sauce!

Cheese sauce?! Yes, you heard right! An unexpected but heavenly combination that took the classic schnitzel to new heights. The creamy sauce gave the crispy breading an extra oomph, and turned the already substantial schnitzel into a true bomb of flavors.

Was it heavy? You bet! But was it delicious? OH YES! Sometimes you have to sacrifice yourself for a good cause, and in this case, the cause was a schnitzel experience beyond the ordinary. Das Zwiespalt, you have won our hearts (and stomachs)!

Berlin, Berlin! Germany's vibrant capital, where history and modern life meet in a beautiful union. But amidst the hustle and bustle of the big city, there are also small oases of tradition and charm.

One of these oases is FAUSTUS SCHNITZELHAUS, located right by the iconic KaDeWe. The name alone made our eyes widen – could this be schnitzel heaven?

And yes, it could! Inside, a world opened up where time seemed to stand still. Dark wood paneling, cozy lighting and an atmosphere of genuine German "gemütlichkeit". Here, on a giant wooden board, we were presented with "Kalbsschnitzel A": a crispy, golden schnitzel, served with a mountain of potatoes, lemon and cranberry marmalade.

The portions were enormous! Even the hungriest giant would have a hard time finishing it. But we fought bravely, and the reward was a belly full of happiness and a feeling of having experienced true Berlin schnitzel magic.

Lübeck, ah Lübeck! This charming Hanseatic city held a very special schnitzel surprise. At Brauberger, a cozy brewhouse with the aroma of malt and hops, we found a schnitzel that was... different.

The secret? The breading! It was made from the grain used to brew the house beer. Recycling at its finest! The result? A unique, rustic, and coarsely grained breading that gave the schnitzel a whole new dimension of flavor and texture.

Imagine the crispy breading crunching between your teeth, while the delicate taste of beer mingles with the tender meat. A true taste experience that made us shout "Prost!" with delight.

Brauberger, you have proven that innovation and tradition can go hand in hand - and the result is a schnitzel worth traveling to Lübeck for!

Poland, you hidden gem! Who would have thought that an anonymous schnitzel in a quiet residential area in Bielsko-Biała could hold such a great taste experience?

"Tulipan", a true local gem, lured us in with its modest facade and authentic atmosphere. Here, far from tourist traps and Michelin stars, we found a schnitzel that was both honest and delicious.

And the price? It was so low that we almost couldn't believe our own eyes! A schnitzel dream come true without breaking the bank.

Tulipan, you have proven that true schnitzel joy doesn't have to cost a fortune. Thank you for an unforgettable taste experience - and for showing us that the best treasures are often found where you least expect them!

Zator, you little Polish charmer! Who knew you were hiding such a unique schnitzel secret?

In Poland, they do things a little differently. Here, a crispy, golden schnitzel is not enough – no, it needs the company of a sour twist! In Zator, we found the schnitzel served with a delightful combination of red cabbage and grated carrots.

And let's just say it as it is: It was a brilliant idea! The sour taste of red cabbage and carrots gave a fresh touch to the rich schnitzel, creating a perfect balance between the heavy and the light.

Zator, you have shown us that the schnitzel universe is full of surprises. Thank you for broadening our horizons - and for giving us a taste experience that was both traditional and innovative at the same time!

Imagine this: Gray, dreary concrete buildings stretching towards the sky like monuments to a bygone era. Soviet architecture in its most brutal form. A place where you least expect to find culinary happiness.

But wait! What is that aroma that suddenly tickles the nostrils? A scent of crispy breading, spiced and golden. We follow the scent, and like an oasis in the concrete desert, it appears: Restaurant Kryształowa.

And here, amidst these dreary surroundings, is served the best schnitzel we have ever tasted! A perfectly breaded beauty, accompanied by freshly roasted potatoes with bacon and onions. A symphony of flavor and texture that makes the angels sing.

Kryształowa, you are proof that true beauty can be found even in the most unexpected places. Thank you for bringing light and joy to an otherwise gray world - and for serving a schnitzel that is a true tribute to taste!

Prague! The city of a thousand spires, the golden beer, and... the questionable schnitzel?

We had heard rumors of Prague's culinary scene, of the sumptuous meals and flavorful experiences. But alas, our first encounter with the Czech schnitzel was a sorry affair.

Lured by signs boasting of "the city's biggest and oldest restaurant", we made the fatal mistake of stepping inside. And what were we met with? Two pathetic, dry schnitzels that looked like something the cat dragged in.

The fries were an equally sad story: lukewarm, limp, and without a grain of salt. A disappointment of epic proportions that made us question Prague's gastronomic reputation.

But don't despair, dear reader! Prague has much more to offer than this one unfortunate experience. We promise to continue the hunt for the perfect schnitzel - and we refuse to let this one setback spoil our culinary adventure!

After the disappointing schnitzel debut in Prague, we were ready for revenge! We ventured far from the tourist traps in the center and found a hidden gem: Vila Kajetánka, a charming restaurant nestled in a beautiful park.

And here, surrounded by green trees and birdsong, we finally found schnitzel happiness! A perfectly golden brown beauty, with a thick and crispy breading that made our mouths water.

The picture may not do it justice, but believe us - this schnitzel was a dream! Served with a fresh and delicious potato salad, it was the perfect antidote to the dry and sad experience from the day before.

Vila Kajetánka, you have redeemed Prague's honor! Thank you for showing us that the Czech capital can certainly conjure up schnitzel magic when you know where to look.

Dresden, you beautiful city on the Elbe! In the middle of the rebuilt Altstadt, with the majestic Frauenkirche as a backdrop, we found a little piece of Bavaria: Restaurant Augustiner.

With its blue-checked tablecloths and cozy atmosphere, it reminded us of the southern German beer halls, where the mood is high and the beer flows freely. And of course, we had to try a schnitzel!

The choice fell on the classic Wiener Art - a sure winner when you're on a schnitzel hunt. And Augustiner did not disappoint! A crispy, golden schnitzel, served with a fresh and tangy potato salad. A true taste experience that made us sing "Ein Prosit!" with delight.

The Germans simply have a handle on their schnitzels! And Augustiner in Dresden is no exception. A perfect combination of coziness, atmosphere and good taste.

Potsdam! Not only do you hold a beautiful palace and a fascinating history, you also house a true Schnitzel-monster!

At REDO XXL, it's not about finesse and elegance. Here the motto is: "Go big or go home!" And when they say "big", they mean it! Our eyes almost popped out of our heads when we saw the gigantic schnitzel on the menu. 600 grams?! That was the small one! For the truly brave or hungry souls, they offer a 2 kg monster of a schnitzel.

We chose the "small" one and must admit that the taste did not quite live up to the size. But hey, sometimes it's not just about the perfect taste experience. Sometimes it just has to be fun, crazy and unforgettable. And REDO XXL certainly was that!

A schnitzel experience beyond the ordinary, which made us laugh, gasp and roll out of there with an overflowing stomach. REDO XXL, thank you for showing us that size sometimes does matter!

Hungary, you land of paprika and goulash! We had high expectations for your schnitzel, but we must admit that we were a little surprised.

This one had a touch of "cutlet" about it. Maybe it was just trying to confuse us? But hey, we're not afraid of a little adventure! And the taste? It was actually good! Crispy breading, tender meat and a lovely spicy flavor.

But wait, what's this? A bone? Yes, you read that right! This schnitzel came with a built-in "handle". Handy if you want to gnaw on it like a caveman! And then there was the mysterious bacon creation... More decoration than enjoyment, but fun to look at.

Hungarian schnitzel, you are a rebel! You don't follow the rules, but you do it with style. Thank you for an unforgettable experience - and for reminding us that the schnitzel universe is full of surprises!

Kiel! This lively port city is not only known for ferries and fresh fish, but also hides a very special schnitzel treasure!

On a rainy Saturday afternoon, where even the seagulls sought shelter, we found comfort in Gaststätte Ratskeller. And yes, you see correctly! Another Ratskeller! These cozy basement restaurants are a sure hit when you're looking for good, old-fashioned German food.

And Kiel does not disappoint! Here we were treated to a crispy and golden schnitzel that made our mouths water. Served with a generous portion of French fries, it was the perfect cure for the gray weather blues.

Ratskeller in Kiel, you are a true schnitzel hero! Thank you for upholding German food culture - and for giving us a taste experience that warms the heart, even on a rainy day.

Lithuania! A land of beautiful forests, charming towns and... a challenge for schnitzel enthusiasts? We have to admit it. Finding a real schnitzel in Lithuania was like looking for a needle in a haystack.

But we didn't give up! In the slightly curious town of Elektrėnai, we found Perkunkiemis plius - a restaurant that promised "European" food. With a certain amount of skepticism, we sat down at the table and immediately felt transported back in time. The two young waitresses didn't speak a word of English, and the menu was a riddle, even for Google Translate.
But with gestures and smiles, we managed to order a "schnitzel". And what did we get? Well, more of a cutlet than a schnitzel, but with a crispy and tasty breading that at least soothed our schnitzel cravings.

Perkunkiemis plius, thanks for trying! You are proof that even in the most unexpected corners of the world, you can find a glimmer of schnitzel hope. And hey, at least it was a fun story to tell!

Kętrzyn, a town with a heavy history! Here, where Hitler's Wolf's Lair still casts long shadows, we found a small oasis of peace and schnitzel joy: the eatery "Cois"!

In the midst of this historic town, with memories of war and destruction, it was a relief to sink our teeth into a crispy and delicious schnitzel. And Cois did not disappoint!

I chose a mushroom and cheese schnitzel that made the good breading sing. A creamy and rich taste experience that made me forget all about war and misery. My companion was more classically inclined and got a schnitzel with a smiling fried egg on top. A sure winner, as always!

Cois, you are proof that even in the darkest of times, good food can bring light and joy. Thank you for a tasty experience - and for giving us a break from the heavy weight of history.

Gdansk! A city with a fascinating history, beautiful architecture and... a schnitzel experience with a twist?

In the old railway station buildings, where trains once brought travelers to and from the city, you will now find PG4 - a restaurant and brewery with an industrial chic look. The place oozes history and atmosphere, and we were excited to see if their schnitzel could live up to the cool surroundings.

And the answer? Well, let's put it this way: The schnitzel was decent. Crispy breading, tender meat, no complaints there. But it was clear that PG4's heart beats more for beer than for food.

Maybe the chef was distracted by the many beer tanks? Maybe the focus was more on creating the perfect IPA than the perfect breading? Either way, it was a bit of a shame. Because with the cool surroundings and the potential that was in the air, PG4 could have served a schnitzel experience beyond the ordinary.

But hey, we got a good story out of it! And who knows, maybe their beer is better than their schnitzel? That has to be a project for another time!

Szczecin, you surprised us! In this Polish port city, with its charming mix of German and Polish culture, we found a small, Czech-inspired eatery that hid a big schnitzel secret.

With a certain amount of skepticism (and a good amount of hunger!) we squeezed into the small, cozy place. Could they possibly accommodate two large, schnitzel-hungry men on a busy Saturday night? The answer was a resounding YES!

And what a schnitzel they served! A crispy, golden brown beauty, with a thick and coarse breading that testified to love and care. You could almost taste the passion the chef had put into every bite.

It's always a pleasure to find those small, hidden gems where attention is paid to the details. The place where food is not just food, but a declaration of love to the taste buds. Szczecin, thank you for showing us that the best schnitzels are often found where you least expect them!

 Sweden! The land of red wooden houses, ABBA and... schnitzel? Well, that's what we were hoping to find in the charming town of Trelleborg anyway.

With joyful anticipation, we stepped into "Restaurang Istanbul" and ordered a schnitzel. But alas, the disappointment was huge! This Swedish version of the beloved classic was a sad affair.

Firstly: Deep fried! A schnitzel should be fried in plenty of butter in a pan, not dipped in a pool of hot oil. Secondly: The size! This "schnitzel" was so small that it would have been considered an appetizer in Vienna.

Restaurang Istanbul in Trelleborg, you have to go back to the drawing board! The Swedes have a lot to learn when it comes to the art of schnitzel. Until then, we'll stick to the German and Austrian masters.

Kalmar! After the disappointing schnitzel debut in Trelleborg, we were a bit skeptical about Sweden's abilities in the art of breading and frying. But we are optimists, so we decided to give Swedish schnitzels another chance!

And where would we find this chance? In a Scottish bar, of course! "Pipes of Scotland" in Kalmar, with tartan patterns and whiskey galore, might not seem like the obvious place for a schnitzel experience. But we were willing to try anything to restore our faith in Swedish schnitzel art.

And wow, what a surprise! This time the schnitzel was pan-fried, just the way it should be. Crispy, golden and full of flavor. And as if that wasn't enough, the potatoes were also fried to perfection. A true feast for the taste buds!

Pipes of Scotland, you have saved the Swedish schnitzel honor! Who would have thought that a Scottish bar in Kalmar could serve a schnitzel that made us forget all about the Trelleborg fiasco? Thank you for proving that Sweden, after all, has the potential to become a schnitzel nation!

Ah, the Danish schnitzel! A classic that brings back memories of childhood Sundays and grandma's cooking. Here you get the real deal, served with love and all the traditional elements: crispy, golden-roasted potatoes, a velvety smooth gravy, and a dollop of fresh peas.

We have, however, chosen to skip the "dreng", the little guy with anchovies and capers, as our taste buds don't quite agree with the salty fish flavor. But fear not! The schnitzel is still a true flavor bomb that makes your mouth water.

One thing that sets the Danish schnitzel apart from its European cousins is the thickness. Here at home, we don't pound the meat quite as flat, which makes for a more substantial and juicy schnitzel experience.

That's precisely what makes the schnitzel universe so exciting! From thin, crispy slices in Vienna to thick, juicy steaks in Denmark - there's a schnitzel for every taste and every mood. And the Danish version? It has a very special place in our hearts and stomachs!

Wrocław! Not only are you a beautiful city with a rich history, you also hide hidden schnitzel gems - even in a hotel restaurant!

Imagine: You check into a cozy hotel on the outskirts of the city. The rain is drumming lightly on the window, and your stomach is rumbling. You decide to try the hotel restaurant, and what do you see on the menu? A schnitzel, of course!

With excitement you wait for your food, and in comes the waiter with a smile, presenting... a schnitzel with a twist! On the plate lies a crispy, golden brown beauty of a schnitzel. But wait! What's hiding underneath? A bed of creamy potato salad peeks out, and on top of the schnitzel sits a fried egg, completing this masterpiece.

The Poles really know how to spoil the taste buds! They take the classic schnitzel and give it a creative twist that takes the taste experience to new heights. Wrocław, you have won our hearts and stomachs with this unexpected schnitzel creation in your hotel restaurant. Thank you for showing us that the schnitzel adventure can be found even in the most unexpected places!

Wrocław, you offer schnitzel adventures in all shapes and sizes! This time the hunt took us to SETKA - Restauracja Polska, a place where you can not only enjoy a good schnitzel, but also a real car show!

Imagine: You sit and enjoy your food while the coolest cars cruise by right outside the window. The roar of the engines mixes with the sound of cutlery against plates, and the smell of gasoline fights for attention with the lovely aroma of breaded meat. A true feast for the senses!

And the schnitzel? It was definitely not a bit player in this show! A crispy, golden brown beauty that made our mouths water. Served with boiled potatoes yes! and a fresh cucumber salad, it was a perfect combination of taste and texture.

SETKA - Restauracja Polska, thank you for an unforgettable experience! You have shown us that schnitzel joy can be combined with the smell of gasoline and the roar of engines - and the result is a true explosion of impressions!

Warsaw! Poland's vibrant heart, where history and modern life meet in an elegant dance. Here, among beautiful buildings and bustling streets, hides a restaurant that will make even the most discerning schnitzel connoisseur's eyes widen: Stary Dom!

Imagine: We step into a world of elegance and refinement. People in evening gowns and suits, subdued lighting and an atmosphere of exclusivity. We might have felt a bit underdressed in our jeans and sneakers, but hey, adventure calls!

And then it arrived: The schnitzel! Served with pomp and circumstance, it lived up to the high expectations. Crispy, golden and perfectly cooked. A true taste experience that came with a price though - the most expensive schnitzel we have ever eaten!

Was it worth the price? Well, that's a question that still haunts us in our dreams. But one thing is certain: We had an unforgettable experience in Warsaw's finest company, and washed the schnitzel down with a beer from Poland's oldest brewery. Sometimes you have to sacrifice a little to experience the extraordinary - and this schnitzel was definitely extraordinary!

This schnitzel is not for the faint of heart! It's gigantic, it's epic, it's... well, it's simply wild! We thought Vienna was the undisputed king of the schnitzel universe, but Podwale 25 Kompania Piwna in Poland has taken the crown with a bang!

Imagine: You walk into a restaurant with an Austrian theme. Checkered tablecloths, waiters in lederhosen, the mood is set. You order a schnitzel, expecting a classic, breaded affair. But then it arrives... a monster of a schnitzel that makes your jaw hit the floor! It covers the entire plate, and you consider for a moment whether to use a knife and fork or a chainsaw.

But fear not! This giant is as delicious as it is big. Crispy, golden and infinitely tasty. A true schnitzel dream that sends you straight to food heaven.

Podwale 25 Kompania Piwna, you took us by surprise! Thank you for an unforgettable schnitzel experience that proves that Poland is not only pierogi and sausages, but also a schnitzel superpower!

"Sour Schnitzel?!?" What in the world is that? After countless schnitzel adventures, we thought we had seen it all. But Kamienica Riaucourt in Poland proved that the schnitzel universe still holds surprises!

This time it wasn't the size or the side dishes that stole the show, but the meat itself. A "sour schnitzel" - an Austrian specialty where the meat is preserved with nitrate salts. The result? A beautiful, pink color and a taste that sent us straight to schnitzel heaven!

Imagine: A crispy, golden breading that embraces a tender and juicy piece of meat with a delicate, sour taste. A taste experience that is both traditional and innovative at the same time.

Kamienica Riaucourt, thank you for expanding our schnitzel horizon! You have proven that even the most experienced schnitzel hunters can always learn something new. And this sour schnitzel? It has secured a place in our schnitzel hearts forever!

A classic Polish motorway restaurant. The smell of fried food and diesel hangs heavy in the air. Truck drivers in clogs without heel caps slurp coffee and discuss the day's hardships. Not exactly a place where you expect to find culinary masterpieces, right?

But hold on tight! Suddenly it appears - a schnitzel of the rare kind! Crispy, golden and breaded to perfection. A true oasis in a sea of sausages and mashed potatoes.

We rubbed our eyes and could hardly believe it. Was it really possible to find such a heavenly schnitzel in an anonymous motorway restaurant between Toruń and Bydgoszcz? The answer was a resounding YES!

While the Polish truck drivers clinked their coffee cups, we sat and enjoyed every bite of this unexpected delicacy. A schnitzel experience that proved that you should never judge a book by its cover - or a restaurant by its location. Because even in the most unexpected places, you can find taste experiences that send you straight to food heaven!

And so we reach the end of our journey! But fear not, dear schnitzel enthusiasts, we're finishing with a bang! A tribute to the Danish schnitzel, the one that always has a special place in our hearts (and stomachs!).

This one is a true classic: Double-breaded, crispy and golden brown. Served with roasted potatoes, still glistening with the blissful fat from the pan. A symphony of taste and texture that sends you straight back to childhood Sundays at Grandma's.

No frills, no fancy accessories. Just an honest, tasty schnitzel that hits the spot every time. Because sometimes it's the simple things that make life the best. And the Danish schnitzel? It's simply unbeatable!

Thank you for joining us on our schnitzel odyssey! We hope you enjoyed the ride and that you have been inspired to go hunting for your own schnitzel happiness. Remember: The world is full of crispy, golden surprises - it's just a matter of finding them!

Made in the USA
Monee, IL
14 July 2025